Whimsical Triumphs

Sonal Saxena

BookLeaf Publishing

India | USA | UK

Presentation by *BookLeaf Publishing*

Web: www.bookleafpub.com

E-mail: info@bookleafpub.com

ISBN: 9789360945725

First edition 2024

To those who never judged my poems for having too many puns, rhymes that don't make sense, or verses longer than anyone's attention span. Your tolerance deserves a standing ovation. This one's for you, my dear readers!

With laughter and endless metaphors,

Sonal

ACKNOWLEDGEMENT

In the whimsical circus of life, nurturing "Whimsical Triumphs" has been my high-flying act, and I've not done it alone!

To my family, who mastered the art of nodding and smiling even when my poetic genius seemed to hardly make sense—your patience deserves an award. Your unwavering encouragement has been the cornerstone of my creative endeavours, thank you for fostering an environment where imagination could flourish. Your love has been the gentle breeze beneath my wings.

To New York, my chaotic yet inspiring muse, where even the pigeons have poetic potential—your streets are my poetic playground.

To the readers, who embark on this poetic rollercoaster with a mix of anticipation and bravery—brace yourselves for a journey filled with laughter, reflection, and perhaps a sprinkle of confusion.

And to poetry itself, my quirky companion to inspire me to the limits that I gathered the courage to use one for my first book.

With laughter and poetic mischief,
Hope you enjoy this Whimsical journey
Sonal

PREFACE

In a delicate tango between words and emotions, this collection of poems emerges as a testament to the beauty found in the ordinary moments of life. Each verse weaves together threads of inspiration drawn from the rich nature and the nuances of our daily existence. As an author deeply entrenched in the rhythm of New York City, I draw upon the pulse of urban life and the serene whispers of nature to craft these poetic reflections.

This book, a compilation of 21 poems, is a journey through the corridors of motivation and humour, fuelled by the diverse experiences that shape our realities. Every poem is a unique melody, resonating with the shared chords of human experience. With a touch of wit and a sense of calling, these verses aim to engage and uplift, offering readers a moment of solace and encouragement.

As I navigate the bustling streets and tranquil parks, I aspire to infuse the written word with the raw essence of life's beauty. My verses echo the desire to wake up the world with the gentle power of poetry, fostering a kinder and more loving reality. I invite you to embark on this poetic journey, where every page holds a message crafted to resonate with the heart and soul.

Being Me

This poem resonates with every laughter-filled
girl with big dreams, just like me.

I am sassy and sweet, proudly I flaunt,
My love for pink is an unbreakable bond.
With a rebel at heart and have courage so full,
Though I often push the doors that are marked as
'pull'.

I dance to the beat of my own drum,
I'll speak my mind, like a guitar's strum.
I refuse to be ruled, I won't be controlled,
I'll fight for my beliefs, and not what's merely
told.

I may be the queen of comic mishaps,
In a day that goes by so serious perhaps.
clearly, I am the queen of giggles and laughter,
Humour is something we are all after.

Yes, I am always lost when reading maps,
But I explore new paths, and try to mend my
own gaps.
My direction of sixth sense never falls,
With courage, I conquer life's daunting sprawls.

I effortlessly turn heads with my unique style,
All eyes on me, I am the star that beguiles.
Even the top designers find themselves muted,
My magnetic pull often earns me the tag of
OOTD. (Genz slang for Outfit Of The Day)

So when you see me, dressed at nine,
in those sparkling shoes and gloves so fine.
You know I am going to have a whole good
time,
I prefer to have some orange juice and lime.

In a supreme combo, I am a blend of fire and
ice,
With a dash of sugar and tad bit of spice.
Unapologetically me, I am Sassy and sweet,
And that's how I'll always be.

Christmas

Celebration of a happy feeling that fills the air
during Christmas time

The moon hangs low like a silver dime,
On frosted fields the shadows climb.
The air is crisp and the stars are bright,
Its' finally December and Christmas night.

Tis' the season of decked up malls,
With stores adorned in festive sprawls.
As the spirit of Christmas spreads its merry,
Lights twinkle from every nook and cranny.

The aroma of cookies, from the oven so warm,
Fills the air with love and charm.
The stockings hang by the chimney with care,
And children dream of gifts to share.

The tree glistens with warmth and light,
As families gather with smiles and delight.
The fire crackles, with the shared stories,
Making memories paired with glories.

It's the time of magic, miracles and cheer,
The merriest season of the year.

The joy of giving, and the love it brings,
Is the true meaning of this special thing.

So, give a cuddle, in this season so bright,
And cherish the blessings, both big and slight.
May your holiday be filled with love and peace,
And may the spirit of Christmas never cease.

Let's raise our glasses, and make a toast,
To this day that we love the most.
For rich or poor or healthy or ill,
Santa is coming with wishes to fulfil.

The New Road

This is a poem to inspire readers to keep
travelling to new destinations and learn from
new experiences. Often a new road can be full of
surprises and a new beginning.

A new road is a kind of self-discovery,
An opportunity to break free from life's
monotony.
Its an awakening to open our minds and hearts,
And truly appreciate world's diverse parts.

These mountains stand as mentors and more,
Seas share their secrets from every distant shore.
With new horizons your insight grows,
Moving places is a tutorial as you know.

From the bustling cities that never sleep,
To tranquil valleys, vast and deep.
Every step I take, a new lesson is learned,
My perception shifts and an experience is
earned.

The pleasure of meeting new people, foods and
cultures,
A chance to explore from unknown adventures.

Embark on a journey to discover and
understand,
Different ways of life in a foreign land.

Taste the spice in distant lands,
Take the pleasure of various ways of shaking
hands.
Feel the rhythm of languages in windswept
chimes,
Learn from their laughter, tears, and rhymes.

The people we meet, their stories we share,
It's a bond of understanding, unique and rare.
All cultures and traditions we should celebrate,
After all, it's a human feeling that resonate.

Through the new roads, my vision expands,
Grasping the world right within my hands.
For in the exploration, I truly find,
A deeper meaning of mankind.

FIRST SNOW

An expression of happiness when I saw the first
Snow in my life

The air is crisp, the world is in awe,
As nature paints a picture, frosty and raw.
A moment frozen in time, a sight so white,
The first snowfall is a magical delight.

Whispers of winter softly blow,
A brand-new song begins with the first snow.
Each flake a symbol, pure and white,
sends a message for us by nature's might.

In the midst of winter with utter cold,
Snowflakes danced on the backyard pole.
From fallen leaves to this bright white sway,
Nature's bringing the change, in its own
charming way.

A peaceful silence, a magical glow,
The first snow is beautiful, now I know.
But we must be cautious we must be wise,
This snow in disguise can even bring an evil
surprise.

Amidst this beauty, danger quietly waits,
cars collides, and roads are like ice for skates.
Our daily routines, hindered and slowed,
First snow is really a double edged sword.

So with every flake that touches the floor,
A lesson lingers, to be cautious while you
explore.
This eternal cycle of life is absolute divine,
When old door shuts, new ones align.

With Each delicate snowflake around,
that lands softly upon the frozen ground.
Transforms the familiar into something new,
A masterpiece of winter, beautiful and profound.

So let's celebrate this day of first snowfall,
And cherish nature's transient call.
A dusting of white in a magical sight,
A winter wonderland with a pure delight.

Princess in You

A joyous poem where a princess reassures every
girl: everyone is a princess and everyone's a
queen too

Once upon a time there was a princess with a
flair,
In a kingdom where magic was filled in the air.
She whispered to all, "Find the magic in you,
If you wish from all your heart, your dreams can
really come true".

Unleash the queen, who lies within you,
Discover your prowess, radiant and true.
Clasp your magic wand, let it be seen,
For everyone's a princess, and everyone's a
queen.

Find your magic that's been waiting so long,
make your own tunes and sing your own song.
Only you hold the keys, to make your dreams
come true,
It's a journey of strength and passion through
and through.

You've got the power with a wand in your hand,

There's magic in all of us, just find your
command.
Find the princess in you, find the queen in you,
Gaze the endless sky, seize the mystic view.

As Rumi says, raise your words not the voice,
For good demeanour is a personal choice.
It is the rain that grows flowers, not the thunder,
So leave no room for a verbal blunder.

And when you wear the crown upon your head,
Lead with empathy, kindness, and finesse.
Rule the kingdom not with command but love
instead,
and make your empire free of stress.

Aurora Beyond the Eclipse

A poem of promise to convey failures don't
exist. You either win or learn.

Like the gentle rain on a parched terrain,
Morning brings hope for every pain.
In the daily downpour of disasters, we face,
Its growth that crafts for us a resilient place.

In life's ocean where failures sail,
Aurora beyond the eclipse is a pleasant detail.
Each failure is a note in soothing tune,
A symphony of lessons, granted as a boon.

Those stumbles are a chance to refine,
It's a journey towards excellence you need to
define.
Scars are not wounds but fables in your own
voice,
Failures lead to victory is one of the timeless
ploys.

In search of a flash, courage find wings,
Aurora beyond the eclipse is where the heart
sings.

Being human and sentimental, is a blend so
bizarre,
This is the last lap of the run and we shouldn't
be far.

So, clinch the eclipse, let shadows depart,
A daybreak awaits you with a generous heart.
Your pearls of struggles are a thing to showcase,
Use them as learnings in the goals that you
chase.

Diet Controls

This poem captures my personal journey and
emotions as I embraced dieting to achieve
fitness and good shape.

It's a moment of truth, a wake-up call,
Your body's telling you to go for an overhaul.
Years of indulgence, now it's time to pay,
I am determined, and I will make my way.

The weighing scale has been unkind and cold,
The jeans that used to fit, now it sadly fold.
A stronger body, a clearer mind,
A better version of myself I am trying to find.

It's not about deprivation,
But a whole new transformation.
A journey to get back in shape,
Making healthy choices that I can't escape.

So I am staying strong and staying committed,
For this goal, that I have admitted.
Stop seeing Dieting as a punishment,
This is a path for my better nourishment.

Counting my daily calories intake,

And closely watch what I eat with no mistake.
No more sinful indulgences,
or this can have harsh consequences.

Keto, Paleo, what's the latest charade?
I am up for a marathon or walk in a parade.
No cakes, no sugar, oh, what a life,
A date with veggies on the edge of a knife.

And then in a few days or so,
Witness me transformed in a fairy tale's glow.
Then don't envy me or pretend to be concerned,
As I'll be making millions of heads turned.

NEW YORK

This poem celebrates the vibrancy and endless
possibilities of New York City, known as a land
of opportunities.

In the heart of dreams, where odds bloom,
New York City, a land where potential loom.
A symphony of chaos, a bustling song,
Where no one judges you right and wrong.

New York is a paradox of beauty and haste,
A vibrant abode with a blingy taste.
Times Square's glow is scintillating and bright,
In its neon glow, many dreams ignite.

Manhattan's streets, are untidy and unclean,
Yet within this chaos there is a lively sheen.
It's a city that never seems to sleep,
Working day and night digging the secrets deep.

You can ache your neck with the towers so high,
Here bridges are so giant it can touch the sky.
Cherry Blossoms in Central Park is stunning to
see,
Whole world comes here in the tourism spree.

From dreamy winters to gritty sidewalks,
I've found my haven in these city blocks.
New York's heart is tough and strong,
With its flaws and perfections now, this is where
I belong.

Divided Lines/Borderlines

This poignant letter reveals the emotional
journey of a mother separated from her son due
to the immigration crisis.

Dear son, my heart aches with sadness, as I pen
this letter to you this hour,
From a separated land of borders, Divided by
politics and power.

Where crowns of silver has turned to grey, and
no one has a real heart,
A world once united is now fractured in pieces
and have torn us apart.

Scales of justice, tipped and swayed, with shouts
of anger and voices raw,
while whispers of corruption loudly displayed,
and inequality undermines the law.

What happened to the leaders of the past?
Who fought for justice, and made it last.

Their voices were soft but stood tall,
Against injustice and greed, for one and all.

Oh, how I long for the days of old,
When love and compassion were worth more
than gold.

Unlike this world where leaders preach of
kindness but divides us with words so sweet,
Their actions are cruel, agendas are hidden, and
they no longer remain elite.

Do you see the games they play,
to manipulate our lives every single day.

Profits and revenue, their utmost prize,
while compassion and humanity slowly dies.

If you challenge their power, they'll make it
clear,
The lines they draw are ones to fear.

So dear son, don't struggle to come and see me,
In this world of chaos, it's not meant to be.

Don't risk yourself crossing these perilous lines,
These deceitful paints may claim precious life
yours or mine.

But if you get a chance, choose who you put in
power,

For they can make or break our future and
influence us every hour.

But my son, unlike these leaders, not all hearts
are fake and phony,
Common people like us are full of love and live
in harmony.

Beyond our religion, color, origin or nationality,
We all are emotional happy souls and that's the
brutal reality.

Don't lose hope as its just a matter of time,
There will soon be another Gandhi, Lincoln or
Mandela with a little chime.

They will bring back the old times for the
unfortunate and the small,
I shall pray that it comes soon, so we can break
these walls.

Till then, Praise the sun, behold the moon,
stretch your arms in our shared skies,
Know that your mother watches you everyday,
from where another horizon lies.

With tear-kissed hand and heart of hopes your
mother writes this line,

Freedom will bloom soon, I will cuddle you
tight, and trust me, everything will be fine.

Idioms

This poem flaunts the charm of using idioms,
and how they enrich your speech with
eloquence.

In conversations, I dance with flair,
In language riddles, you'll find me there.
Cats and curiosity painted a charming delight,
I add colours in speech with a wee bit of insight.

In simple terms, I faced a difficult task,
But with an idiom, I put on a brave mask.
"Turning over a new leaf," I joyfully proclaim,
Making tittle tattles into a flourishing game.

In plain words, they may judge you mild,
But with idioms, you become linguistically wild.
From the mediocrity, you eloquently ascend,
Using idioms, you're a sought-after blend.

With idioms stars twinkle more at night,
The grass looks greener in every sight.
The sun shines brighter than it really does,
And even rain becomes a melodious buzz.

So spend in reading and downsize your fries,

Use some idioms and show you're wise.
A penny for your thoughts if someone says,
Just break the ice and cut to the chase.

Living away from Home

This poem deeply connects with all those who
are living away from their families, portraying
the conflict between the mind and heart.

If world could be squeezed into a tiny space,
I could cross miles and miles and keep up with
the pace.

Living away from home is bittersweet, at times,
I long for the comfort but still crave for our
climbs.

I toil each day, yet struggle to find peace,
The constant ache of missing home never tend to
cease.
Talking only on phones is a continuous quandary
I face,
Two places I call home, but neither feels like my
only place.

This travelling on flights makes me always
stressed,
I learn and grow in both these places, so I feel I
am blessed.

I miss my parents' house, where I grew up and
learned to be me,
But this city fuelled me to chase my dreams
becoming wild and free.

I long for the comfort and safety of my
childhood nest,
But the thrill of exploration and independence
keeps me on this quest.

I've made new friends and countless memories
along my way,
But that pull of going home is strong, every
single day.

In this endless struggle, I find my heart's refrain,
I belong to both, to neither, or yet I remain.

Which place is truly mine, I always wonder,
A never-ending puzzle I often ponder.

I wish that time and space would bend and blur,
So we could never miss any special moments to
occur.

I'd travel through the skies, or swim across the
sea,
To be with my mom, and enjoy the family spree.

But until that day may come, I'll hold on to this journey long,
To the memories of home and keep my spirit strong.

Colors around You

A beautiful poem to learn not from someone but
from the colors around you.

The colors of life, are vibrant and bright,
It reflects the beauty of our human sight.
From the rose-tinted dawn to the sunset glows,
Each color is a story, as unique as it shows.

The azure of the sky is serene and high,
It inspires us to reach for the heavens and fly.
The green of the trees is so lush and strong,
Teaches us to slowly grow all day long.

The purple of lavender, so delicate and fine,
Encourages us to be gentle, and kind.
White in the clouds they mirror our dreams in a
view,
As we strive for laughter, and look for
something new.

Violet is for creativity, to let our minds explore,
To enjoy the dance of imagination and let the
world adore.
The crimson of roses, so passionate and whole,
Inspires us to love, with all our heart and soul.

The yellow of sunflowers brings secret
encounters,
Reminds us to smile, and take care of others.
The orange of sunsets is fiery and grand,
Fills us with some spice, in this world so bland.

Turquoise portrays the calm and the peace
within,
Indigo is for intuition, to trust your own skin.
Gold is radiant portraying luxury and fragile,
Silver with its moonlit glow, tells us to be stylish
and agile.

Black whispers mystery while grey offers depth,
In shades of darkness, nature's secrets are well
kept.
Orange ignites that view while ivory destroys all
fear,
Maroon fills you with dreams and Pink brings
you a cheer.

Imagine all these are not colors, but people with
thoughts,
Teaching lessons of life and connecting the dots.
In their diversity, an opus crafted with care,
Highlighting our existence with the various
colors to share.

So, Celebrate the rainbow of colors, both bold
and serene,
For in their unique advice, unity can be seen.
Open your eyes and listen to these wise colors,
With a new perspective, there is so much to
discover.

A Better World

A limerick to inspire each one of us and request
for world peace.

I see a light in the darkest night,
For a better world, where all can thrive.
To bring hope for a world that's bright,
This is my dream that keeps me alive.

Where borders are closed and walls are high,
Refugees are living scary and sleepless nights.
Many hopes are shattered beneath the sky,
And every nation outrightly tussles and fights.

Ukraine and Russia fighting in despair,
Where women and children had to flee in
trauma.
Hamas and Gaza filled the cries in the air,
Only the innocent suffered in this political
drama.

Political storms brew constant unrest,
Religious conflicts fuels the flames of hate.
Inequality is on the rise putting nations to test,
Crime, poverty, hunger and Corruption is
ascending in its fastest rate.

Yet in this chaos, I prepare my voice,
for a gentle request and a reminder to pause.
I wrote this poem with some words so fierce,
For a call to action to revisit our cause.

Let's step back and ponder in every space,
Why are we here, on this precious Earth?
This rush of life should not cloud our face,
We are here to heal, to love, and give earth its
worth.

For every child who cries in fear on the edge,
For every family without a home that can stand.
Please join with me today and take a pledge,
we will bestow each a helping hand.

We can rekindle the world where hearts are free,
No matter the color, religion or where we're
from.
Borders disappear, and kindness becomes the
key,
No one sleeps hungry or left in a storm.

If you aint by my side in this journey of swing,
I won't be afraid, I won't back down.
For my conscious poems will continue to sing,
And linger like your favourite song all over the
town.

I'll convince you all, with every word I write,
This mission is ours, not just an invite.
My words and my pen, are here to ignite,
A passion for change and will make you excite.

Through rhythm and rhyme, I see a world
divine,
I am a small Indian girl with a fantasy of delight.
If we all play our part, and take it as a melody to
refine,
A symphony of hope can illuminate the darkest
night.

Seize the Day

This sonnet is inspired by some famous lines by
influencers all over the world. An interesting
way to transform our life by learning from them.

"Only a life lived for others is a life
worthwhile",
Einstein's famous words are still true and
versatile.
A meaningful journey, where selflessness is the
style,
In every act of kindness, our true essence smile.
Credits: Albert Einstein

Maya Angelou always believed in "Still I Rise",
"Try to be a rainbow in someone's cloud".
In adversity's face, your spirit defies,
Leading with kindness will make you proud.
Credits: Maya Angelou

In a fantasy of world, where magic play,
Walt Disney's words lights up our way.
"If you can dream it, you can do it," they always
say,
With imagination, you can seize the day.
Credits: Walt Disney

"Be the change you wish to see",
Are those humble words that sets you free.
Gandhi's wisdom as father of our nation,
Built this country and our very foundation.
Credits: Mahatma Gandhi

Beneath the trees of struggle, where hardships
are sown,
Churchill's words echo a resilient tone.
Like no obstacles can impede the river from
flowing,
"If you are going through hell, just keep going".
Credits: Wincent Churchill

It's not what you have on the outside that glitters
in light,
So don't be afraid to speak up and have no
fright.
Its only then you could make a mark,
It's what you have on the inside that shines in
the dark .
Credits: Anthony Liccione

All that is gold does not glitter,
Not all those who wander are lost.
The old that is strong does not wither,
Deep roots are not reached by the frost.
Credits : J.R.R Tolkein

With every failure, you'll learn to move faster,
Persistence pays to let you learn and become a master.
With every hurdle, you'll gain strength to conquer,
And as they say – "What doesn't kill you makes you stronger".
Credits: Kelly Clarkson

Whimsical Triumphs

This poem is about finding joy in the little things
and seeing the humor and beauty in everyday
life. Embrace the unexpected, laugh at yourself,
and celebrate the small victories - that's the spirit
of a whimsical triumph!

Our life is like a river, with many twist and
turns,
Reveals an enigmatic message, in every step it
churns.
The sunshine after rain, prompts you for happy
jumps,
Add some laughter to your tears and that's called
whimsical triumphs.

We stumble and fall, we pass and we flunk,
But a bad idea is to immerse yourself in sadness
junk.
Add a dash of humour, let some joy be
exchanged,
No matter how much you cry, the past can never
be changed.

Failed to bake a fancy cake is chance to laugh
and share,

Burnt toast for breakfast reminds you that joy is
everywhere.
A wrong exit taken, don't you fear my friend,
A new scenic spot could be just around the bend.

A missed train, due to heavy rain and shade,
Is a hidden triumph that's serenely made.
This is not a loss, but a journey slightly delayed,
In these hidden pauses, silent victories are laid.

A promotion that you may tirelessly dream,
But perhaps it's a nudge, to work with your
team.
To build relationships, to learn and grow,
Until your hard work begins to show.

If conceiving proves a challenge, and leaves you
feeling sad,
Consider it a cue to cherish your youth, be
grateful and glad.
Enjoy this freedom of time before phase of
motherhood,
As it is a transformative journey, shaping your
love for good.

Whimsical triumphs, oh how they play,
With our lives, in their own mischievous way.
A hidden hundred-dollar bill is a forgotten
treasure,

found in an old coat pocket brings an
unexpected pleasure.

A rainbow shimmering, after a sudden
downpour,
An abrupt nature's beauty, leaving us wanting
more.
Serendipity smiles on old friends with grins,
Reunited by chance where a love story could
begin.

Unexpected compliments from the strangers on
the go,
Is a boost to our spirits for a warm, happy glow.
In life's mundane moments, they bring a spark,
A reminder to enjoy the bliss in our hearts.

So, laugh at yourself, with all your might,
Find humour in the scariest of night.
In being whimsical, there's a shining light,
A triumph that makes everything feel right.

Lose like a Winner!

An interesting way to look at your losses and
behave so you can learn and rebound for a
bigger win.

Lose like a winner with grace and charm,
Keep your spirit nice and warm.
Just because defeat has knocked your door,
Doesn't mean the war is lost forevermore.

Lose like a winner with a heart so true,
Congratulate your opponent and show respect
before adieu.
It's time to keep your head high even in the face
of dismay,
Coz, you gave your best today but somehow it
was not your day.

Lose like a winner coz, there is always a lesson
to learn,
In every defeat, a chance to grow and a fire to
burn.
The greatest player has also stumbled while
playing her game,
But champions use these moments like a fire to a
flame.

To lose like a winner is to understand,
that stumbling blocks are a way take command.
Breakdown lessons pave the road to gain,
and set up that courage to bear the pain.

To lose like a winner, it means to ignite,
To burn the fire of resilience long and bright.
For true champions know how to rebound,
With each defeat, a new strength is found.

Lose like a winner, let strength define your fall,
Real losing is in not attempting the call.
Hesitation and fear are natural in a brawl,
The worst defeat isn't in failing, but not trying at
all.

Lose like a winner, with no fear,
When the odds are against you, and the end
seems near.
In the face of defeat, your true character shines,
That is the greatest victory of all times.

Climate Crisis

A wake-up call for each one of us to save the
planet from Climate crisis.

The climate is calling let's hang on and reply,
For the love for our Earth, we need to attend its
cry.
From mountains so high, to the depths of the
seas,
We need to protect the homes of our birds and
the bees.

The world is heating, the ice caps are melting,
Our planet is shifting, the signs are telling.
Plant more trees, and clean the air,
Let's show the Earth, how much we care.

Smoke out of vehicles, releasing gas emissions,
It's time to start taking some eco-friendly
decisions.
Walk, bike, or carpool, to control air pollution,
Let's work together and think of a sustainable
solution.

Pause the use of plastics, save our innocent seas,

In the cleaner air, let the wildlife inhale with
ease.
Abnormal fertilizers, releases methane and
nitrous gases,
Let's switch to organic, and preserve the
meadows and masses.

Hope these verses reaches all our hearts and
minds,
There is an urgency to change, for the entire
humankind.
Sustain the earth, stop the selfish sleaze,
Reduce, reuse, recycle, use this thumb rule
please.

Authorities must take major actions,
To protect our planet and its attractions.
With every choice, be that nature's allies,
Together we'll thrive, and our hope never dies.

To find innovative solutions, we must try,
Reduce our carbon footprint with no deny.
So join me in this mission, and let's do our part,
To heal our beloved Earth, with all our soul and
heart.

Create a safer world, for generations to come,
Our every small step will have a significant
outcome.

Let's make that difference and take one step at a
time,
To restore our planet in a journey sublime.

AI

A cute conversation at length between a girl and
her grandmother on the possibilities with AI.

Hey Grandma, you know, there is a new marvel
called AI,
Which can read thousands of books, in a blink of
an eye.
It never feels bored of reading and can swiftly
scan,
A capability beyond you and I can understand.

These alarms for your medicine that siri and
alexa reminds,
Are now things of the past and far behind.
Your smart phones to millions of appliances,
AI in our lives is becoming a necessary alliance.

These lights to our blinds, they're now so smart,
Making life more convenient, like a work of art.
We are now in the era of tech and machines,
AI is now intertwined in our daily routines.

You know, now the cars can drive us by,
With no drivers at all, and yes this isn't a lie.
Technology is advancing in every stream,

And this is no longer a sci-fi dream.

I am hearing AI can do medical surgeries,
Aiding doctors to diminish their perjuries.
We will soon get our groceries delivered to us,
Seamlessly by AI robots without a fuss.

But, grandma what I am really waiting for is,

When AI could find a cure for you,
And make your knees, as good as new.
You can then run and jump, and dance with glee,
And laugh and love and play with me.

I am waiting when this AI could read my mind
so strong,
tell mommy all the gifts I always long.

And when these robots, so sharp and clever,
Could write my exams with no studies ever.

And grandma, wouldn't it be grand,
If AI can give a tiny plane in my hand?
To zoom and zip to lands of chime,
Within a blink and a snap of time.

But sometimes a weird thought also crosses my
mind,

As it shows in the fictional movies of many
kind.
Can AI take over humans and make us slaves,
Don't know, with mind and power how it
behaves.

Grandma smiles and says with a twinkle in her
eyes,
Glad for love she gets from this young girl so
wise.

"My dearest girl, let me share with you,
The beauty of dreams, both old and new.
While AI may hold wonders untold,
There's magic in your own heart, as pure as gold.

Cherish our inner core that's bound by ties
strong,
And its in that human connection where we truly
belong.

These exams, my love, are paths to explore,
To learn and grow, take no pressure but seek
something more.
For knowledge and wisdom are treasures to find,
In the beautiful journey of an eager mind".

And as for flying, dear one, let me impart,

The wonder of imagination is in the gliding
heart.
Take the scenic route to make memories and
forget the dime,
For the beauty lies not in a snap of time".

Your sweet talks, curiosity so bright,
Are treasures no machine can emulate with
might.
Your laughter, your voice, those innocent calm,
That sets you apart, like a rare precious charm.

Darling, you must overcome your challenges on
earth,
For in your struggles lies your true worth.
Your battles, your triumphs and your unique
fears,
Are elements that make you stand out among
your peers.

AI, a wondrous creation, that is so true,
it can offer help in all that we do.
But don't rely on AI, solely on your way,
For it cannot replace, your own unique way.

I know it's tempting, to let AI take the lead,
But don't forget, it's us the humans who planted
that seed.
We must use it to enhance, not replace,

For our humanity should never be erased.

So, Let's wish that AI with its helping hand,
Can eradicate many illnesses with its magic
wand.
All risky jobs could be done with a sigh,
and no human life will even be sacrificed.

I dream of a future, where AI can bring,
A touch of kindness, to every living being.
No more hate, or discrimination,
Just love and harmony, in every nation.

So, my girl, dream with me, beneath the sun,
Of things AI can make one by one.
For in this race, of man and machine,
We must be wise, to keep the balance clean.

To-Be MOM

This is a feeling when your life changes from
being a normal human to be would-be mother.
An adorable way to accept the changes
happening to you.

Any sugars and chocolates outside? Tell them to
hide!
In a whirlwind of nausea, I am on a rollercoaster
ride.
No gymming, no swimming, took my world by
storm,
Yes, you are right. Here I am now, a 'To-Be'
Mom.

Cravings strikes, from dawn to night,
Ice cream and pickles are such a delight.
Heartbeats are fast, nerves are on a spree,
Clearly, new adventures await for me!

With jitters, baby flutters, and a growing belly so
round,
Nurturing every moment of this new life coming
around.
When my back constantly hurts and these feet
always swell,

I hope its a celestial promise, that all will go
well.

In this delusion of stress and pleasure combined,
I pray for a future be nice and kind.
It's an amusing journey of giggles and tear
rhyme,
As a Mom to be, I am stepping into a whimsical
paradigm.

Global Unity

This is an appeal to every human being to stay
united and make our differences our unique
strength.

The air we breathe, the water we drink,
and which colour runs through our veins you
think.
Our eyes, our hearts, our touch, our smell if all
that is same,
I question our conflict from where it came.

United we stand, divided we fall,
A saying being taught since I was half a feet tall.
Then why those in power fail to understand,
Life's all about sticking together till the end.

We have conquered the roads, and acquired the
skies,
Measured the depth of the oceans where mystery
lies.
We can even challenge death and engineer birth,
But then why humans are defeated by humans
on Earth.

How strong is this religion that pulls us apart,

How harsh is this wealth that has stopped tearing
our heart.
Can a man of a colour be saved from an illness,
Or any gender can dictate your worth or
willingness.

What has made our hearts so tough and eyes to
dry,
Why It has stopped to bothers the voice of a
child cry.
If you call yourself a believer in the religion of
God's bliss,
Tell me which religion teaches to blindly ignore
this.

Ever noticed the birds and the animals,
what makes them always live and sing without
any quarrels.
They know no discrimination, whether you are
from south or north,
They chirp together, fly together and realize
everyone's worth.

Humans could learn a thing or two,
From these creatures, so pure and true.
They teach us to love without any prejudices,
Celebrate the differences and let go of these
malpractices.

No matter our differences, we are all the same,
Overcome hate should be our only aim.
Diversity is our strength to know our knacks,
to prevent ourselves falling through the cracks.

Can you break down the walls, and mend the
bridges,
For a world united, is where everyone has
privileges.
Humanity without division is a dream come true,
With empathy and compassion, we'll make it
through.

It's a heartfelt plea from one human to another,
Stop putting others from smoke into smother.
celebrate our uniqueness with joining hand,
And restore this world to make it grand.

Little Baby Girl

Words cannot describe the feeling when I saw
you.

And Finally, here you are, my little wish from
sky,
I can't stop looking at you, even if I want to try.
As you are born today, my smile is on gleams,
You are the biggest magic from my sweetest
dreams.

With you my pretty angel, my motherhood
begins,
Your chubby cheeks are lovely and how soft is
your skin.
With your golden tears and that cheerful smile of
chrome,
You've just turned my ordinary house into a real
home.

These tiny fingers, and your tiny toes,
who can miss your perfect little nose.
As the doctor heard your first little crackle,
I froze for minutes to see this miracle.

I look forward for the moments, so serene and
new,
to hold you close and spend time with you.
The world welcomes you for the joys big and
small,
And I can't help but feel like the luckiest of all.